Book's Learning Ladders

A Place in Space

WORLD
BOOK

www.worldbook.com

World Book, Inc.
180 North LaSalle Street
Suite 900
Chicago, Illinois 60601
USA

For information about other World Book publications, visit our website at **www.worldbook.com** or call **1-800-WORLDBK (967-5325)**.

For information about sales to schools and libraries, call **1-800-975-3250 (United States); 1-800-837-5365 (Canada)**.

Library of Congress Cataloging-in-Publication Data for this volume has been applied for.

World Book's Learning Ladders
ISBN 978-0-7166-7945-5 (set, hc.)

A Place in Space
ISBN 978-0-7166-7950-9 (hc.)

Also available as:
ISBN 978-0-7166-7960-8 (e-book)

Printed in China by Shenzhen Wing King Tong Paper Products Co, Ltd., Shenzhen, Guangdong
1st printing December 2017

Photographic credits: Cover: NASA/JPL/Space Science Institute; NASA: 4, 8, 11, 13, 14, 16, 17, 18, 22, 23; Portrait of Johannes Kepler (1610), Kremsmünster: 26; © Shutterstock: 6, 8, 12, 20, 27.

Illustrators: WORLD BOOK illustrations by Quadrum Ltd

What's inside?

This book tells you about our solar system. Find out about each of the eight different planets—from Mercury to Neptune. You'll even learn about the sun and how the planets travel around this star.

The solar system

Our **sun** is the star at the center of our solar system.

The solar system is our place in space. The solar system is made up of the sun and the planets and other things that travel around the sun. The word *solar* means *from or of the sun.*

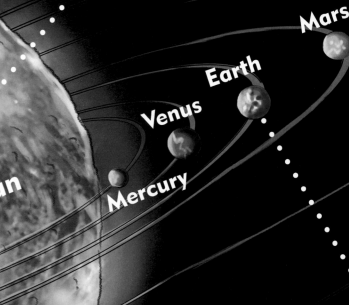

Sun

Mercury

Venus

Earth

Mars

Asteroids, comets, and **meteoroids** are chunks of rock or metal much smaller than planets. They travel around the sun, too.

Scientists called • • • • • • • • • • • • • • •
astronomers explore
and study our solar
system.

Neptune

Uranus

Saturn

Jupiter

Earth, where
we live, is the
third planet
away from the
sun.

There are eight
planets in our
solar system
that travel
around the sun.

It's a fact!

Our solar system began as a huge
spinning cloud of gas. Gas
is something that is not
a liquid, like water, or a
solid, like rock. There
were bits of rock and
metal in the cloud. The bits
banged into one another. The bits
stuck together and started to form
planets.

The Sun

From Earth the sun looks like a giant ball of fire. The sun gives us light, heat, and energy. Almost all living things on Earth—plants, animals, people—need energy from the sun to live. The sun is a thing called a star. There are many, many more stars like our sun in outer space.

The outside of the sun has a temperature of about 10,000 °F (5500 °C)!

Sunspots are dark, circular areas on the outside of the sun.

Plants use light from the sun to make their own food.

Large loops of gas can shoot out of the sun during a bright **solar flare**.

It's a fact!

The sun is about 93 million miles (150 million kilometers) away from Earth. Any closer and our planet would be too hot for us to live on it. Any farther away and it would be too cold.

Mercury

Mercury *(MUR kyuhr ee)* is the planet closest to the sun. It travels around the sun fastest of all the planets. Mercury is also the smallest planet. It is a little larger than Earth's moon. It is hard to see Mercury from Earth without a telescope. A telescope is a tool that makes faraway objects seem closer and bigger.

The United States sent a spacecraft named MESSENGER to Mercury in 2004. From 2011 to 2015, MESSENGER flew around and around Mercury, sending pictures of the planet back to scientists on Earth.

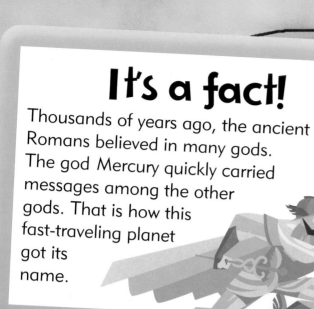

Mercury is a small, rocky planet covered in **craters** (holes).

Mercury is dry, very hot, and has almost no **air.** Air is a mix of gases that we cannot see, smell, or taste.

The **surface** (top layer) has wide, flat areas of land and steep cliffs.

Venus

The planet Venus *(VEE nuhs)* is Earth's closest neighbor in the solar system. Venus and Earth are called twins because they are about the same size.

It's a fact!

The temperature on Venus is higher than that of any other planet.

Venus looks like a bright, yellow object in the sky.

The thick **clouds** that wrap Venus are poisonous.

Most of the land on Venus is smooth and flat. But there are **mountains** and **valleys** there, too.

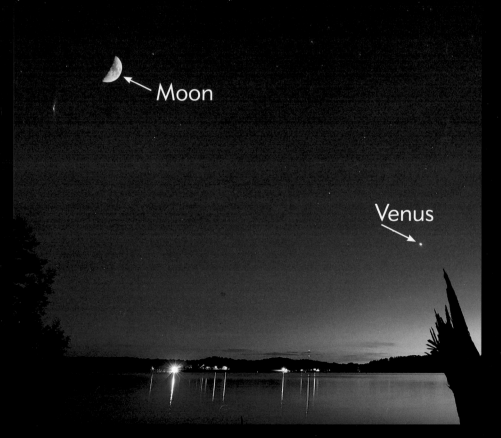

Moon

Venus

Below the clouds, Venus has a rocky, solid **surface**.

Seen from Earth, Venus looks brighter than any other planet or even any star in the night sky.

Earth

Earth *(urth)* is the planet we live on. It is always moving. Earth spins like a top while it travels around the sun. This spinning causes day and night. One day is the time it takes Earth to spin around one time. One year is the time it takes Earth to travel around the sun one time.

The air that surrounds Earth is called the **atmosphere.**

It's a fact!

Earth Day is celebrated on April 22. It is a special day set aside every year to remind people to take care of our environment and all the things on Earth that support life—the air, water, and land.

Almost all of Earth's water is in its **oceans.** Every living thing needs water, like these dolphins. Earth is the only planet that we know of in our solar system with living things.

Most of Earth's surface is covered by **water.**

Earth's **moon** travels around Earth the way that Earth travels around the sun.

The moon looks smooth, but it has rough, rocky **craters**.

U.S. **astronauts** Buzz Aldrin (shown) and Neil A. Armstrong were the first people on the moon, in 1969. They brought moon rocks back to Earth!

Mars

Mars *(mahrz)* is the fourth planet from the sun. It is nicknamed "the Red Planet" because of its color. The ancient Romans thought the planet looked bloody or angry. So they named it after their war god, Mars.

It's a fact!

Mars has two small moons. They are named Phobos *(FOH buhs)* and Deimos *(DY mos)* after sons of the ancient Greek god of war.

The United States sent a huge **rover** nicknamed Curiosity to Mars in 2012. A rover is a vehicle that explores other planets. Curiosity travels on the surface of Mars, sending information about the planet back to scientists on Earth.

Scientists think there may be some water just under the **surface** of Mars.

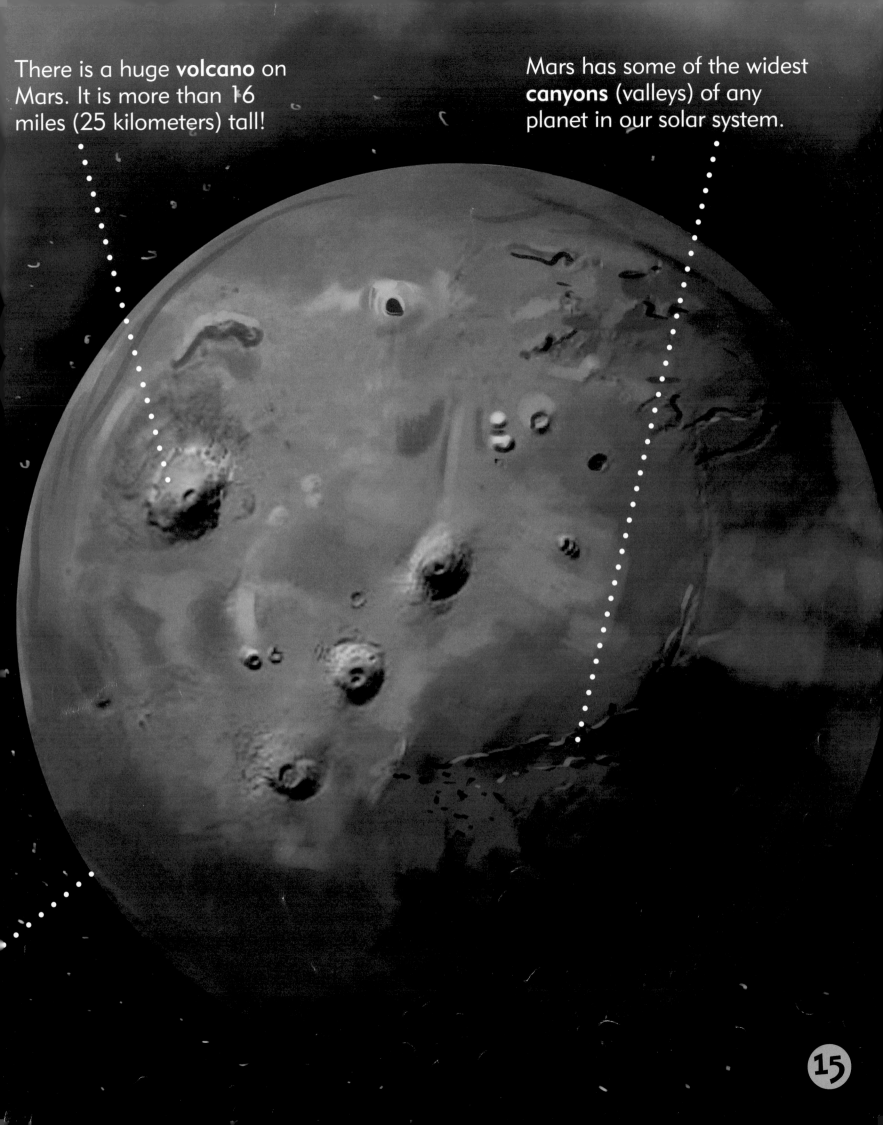

There is a huge **volcano** on Mars. It is more than 16 miles (25 kilometers) tall!

Mars has some of the widest **canyons** (valleys) of any planet in our solar system.

Jupiter

Jupiter *(JOO puh tuhr)* is the biggest plant in the solar system. It is bigger than all the other planets put together! Jupiter is not made of rock like Earth is. Jupiter is made up of thick clouds of gas.

U.S. scientists sent a spacecraft named Juno to study the planet Jupiter. It took Juno almost five years to travel from Earth to Jupiter!

Jupiter is made up of thick red, brown, yellow, and white **clouds of gas.**

It's a fact!

There are thunderstorms on Jupiter. Spacecraft flying past Jupiter have taken pictures of flashes of lightning.

Jupiter has thin **rings** around its middle. The rings are made up of small pieces of dust.

The color of the **Great Red Spot** changes from dark-red to brownish.

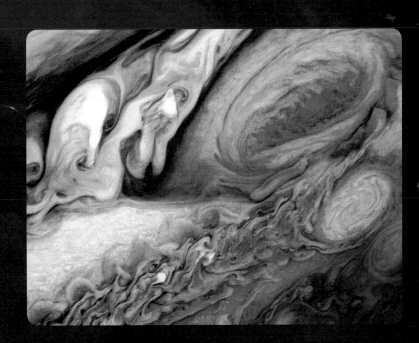

In the clouds that make up Jupiter there is an oval, or roundish, place called the Great Red Spot. Winds spinning fast in Jupiter's clouds cause the spot.

Saturn

Saturn *(SAT uhrn)* is the second largest planet in the solar system. Like Jupiter, Saturn is a huge spinning cloud of gas. It does not have any solid ground. Around Saturn are seven flat rings made of little bits of shiny ice. Saturn's nickname is "the jewel of the solar system" because of its beautiful rings.

Scientists have found many **moons** of different sizes traveling around Saturn. Titan, one of Saturn's moons, is larger than the planet Mercury. There may be an ocean of water inside Titan.

Rings spin around the planet.

Saturn looks like it is wrapped in **bands** because it has clouds of different colors.

It's a fact!

The Italian scientist Galileo (*gal uh LAY oh*) was the first person to see Saturn's rings. In 1610, he looked at Saturn through one of the first telescopes made.

Uranus

The planet Uranus *(YUR uh nuhs)* is the seventh planet away from the sun. Uranus is about four times as big as Earth. The planet is named for an ancient Greek god of the sky.

Scientists think Uranus has a rocky **center,** like Earth does.

British astronomer William Herschel found Uranus in the night sky in 1781. It was the first planet to be found from Earth using a **telescope.** This person is using a modern telescope.

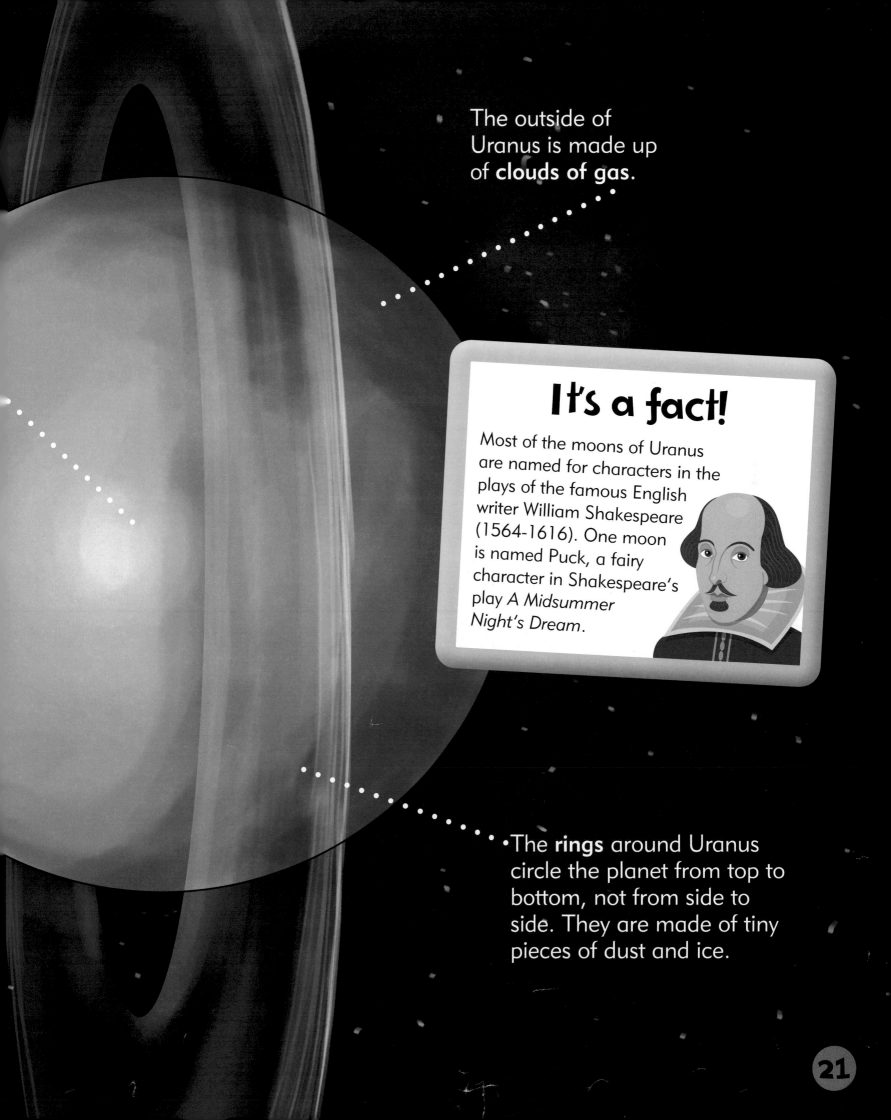

The outside of Uranus is made up of **clouds of gas**.

It's a fact!

Most of the moons of Uranus are named for characters in the plays of the famous English writer William Shakespeare (1564-1616). One moon is named Puck, a fairy character in Shakespeare's play *A Midsummer Night's Dream*.

The **rings** around Uranus circle the planet from top to bottom, not from side to side. They are made of tiny pieces of dust and ice.

Neptune

Neptune *(NEHP toon)* is the planet farthest away from the sun in our solar system. From Earth, we need to use a telescope to see Neptune in the night sky.

Neptune's outer **ring** has five curved areas called arcs that are brighter and thicker than the rest of the ring.

It's a fact!

It takes Neptune 165 years to travel around the sun one time.

Neptune is a very windy planet. High winds blow Neptune's thick clouds at speeds up to 900 miles (1,450 kilometers) per hour!

Because the **clouds** all around Neptune are blue, the planet was named for the ancient Roman god of the sea, Neptune.

Triton, one of Neptune's moons, is unusual. It travels around Neptune in the opposite direction that Neptune moves. Triton is shown in the foreground.

At the planetarium

A field trip to the planetarium *(PLAN uh TAIR ee uhm)* is like an adventure to outer space! A planetarium is a building with a curved ceiling on which lights are flashed to show the movements of objects in the universe. What cosmic objects do you see?

Can you find Earth's moon?

24

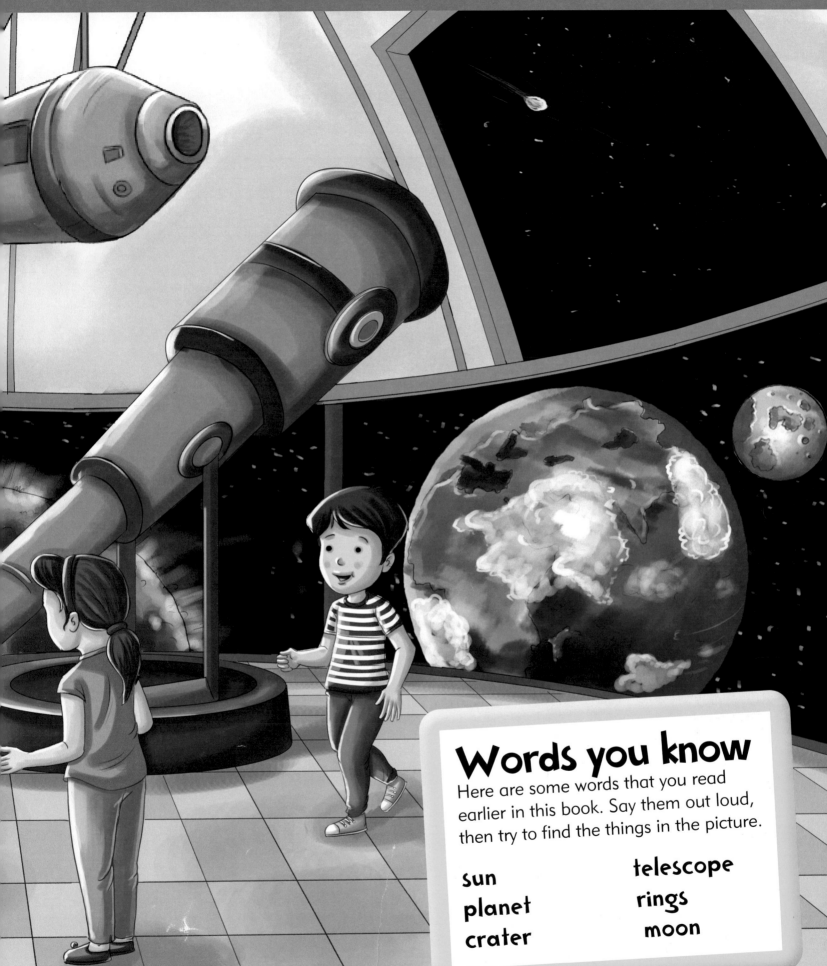

How many planets have rings?

Words you know

Here are some words that you read earlier in this book. Say them out loud, then try to find the things in the picture.

sun   telescope

planet   rings

crater   moon

25

Did you know?

Some scientists use huge telescopes to look into space. But you can see far into space using a simpler and smaller telescope.

Johannes *(yoh HAHN uhs)* Kepler (1571-1630) discovered why the planets travel around the sun the way they do. He figured out the laws of planetary motion.

Light moves really fast— 186,282 miles (299,792 kilometers) in one second! But space is so huge that the light from the sun still takes eight minutes to reach us here on Earth.

A galaxy (*GAL uhk see*) is a giant area of stars, gas, dust, and other bits in space. Our solar system is in the Milky Way galaxy. Our sun is one of billions of stars in the Milky Way.

When astronauts travel into space, they need to wear space suits and helmets. These special suits protect them from the very hot and very cold temperatures in outer space.

In 2006, scientists decided that Pluto was not big enough to be called a planet. So, Pluto became a dwarf planet. And our solar system went from nine to eight planets!

Puzzles

Close-up!

We've zoomed in on three pictures from this book. Guess from the close-up what the whole picture is.

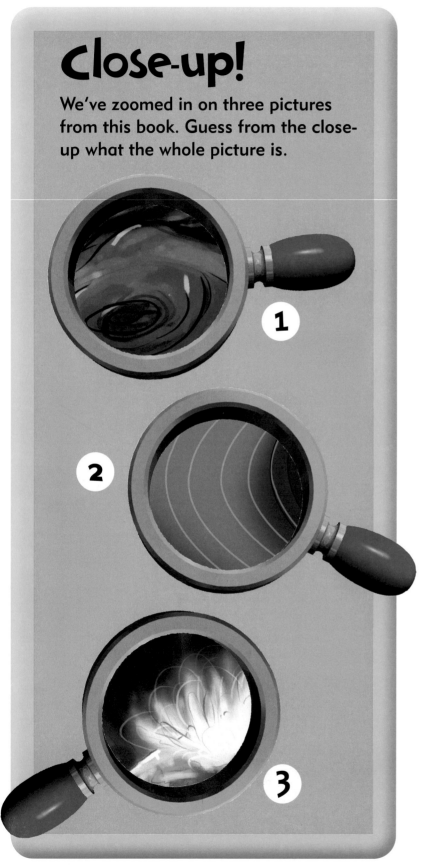

Answers on page 32.

Word jumble!

We've taken words from the book and mixed up the letters. Can you unscramble the letters to identify the words?

1. rsoal tsmyes

2. ctrrae

3. mono

4. ngris

5. glnihgtni

6. utstaron

Match up!

Match each word on the left with its picture on the right.

1. star

2. rover

3. telescope

4. mountain

5. spacecraft

6. Mars

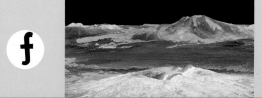

True or false

Can you figure out which of these statements are true? Go to the page numbers given to help you find the answers.

3 Earth is the center of the solar system. **Go to page 4.**

1 Earth is the planet that travels fastest around the sun. **Go to page 8.**

4 The sun is the only star there is. **Go to page 6.**

2 The planet Saturn has no solid ground. **Go to page 18.**

5 Uranus was the first planet to be found from Earth using a telescope. **Go to page 20.**

Answers on page 32.

Find out more

Books

How Many Planets Circle the Sun? by Mary Kay Carson (Sterling Publishing, 2014)
Take a trip into outer space to learn about the asteroid belt, Martian volcanoes, dwarf planets, and other fascinating facts about our universe.

Space Encyclopedia by David A. Aguilar (National Geographic Society, 2013)
This tour of outer space explores the solar system as well as stars, galaxies, and the birth of planets, and speculates on whether other intelligent beings exist in the universe

Star Light, Star Bright: Exploring Our Solar System by Anna Prokos (Red Chair Press, 2017)
Have you ever laid on the ground at night looking up at the twinkling stars? Imagine what it must be like to zip through space and look back to Earth where kids around the globe are gazing into the night sky!

Ultimate Space Atlas by Carolyn DeCristofano (National Geographic Society, 2017)
This out-of-this-world atlas takes readers through maps of the solar system, the Milky Way, and deep space, giving them a close look at and locations of planets, supernovas, and other universes.

Websites

NASA Kids' Club
http://www.nasa.gov/audience/forkids/home/index.html
This NASA website designed for children features information on astronomy and space exploration.

NASA Solar System 101
https://solarsystem.nasa.gov/kids/index.cfm
This NASA website offers an introduction to the solar system, complete with basic facts, illustrations, games, and activities. It also features a page for K-4 kids.

NASA Space Place
http://spaceplace.nasa.gov/en/kids/
You'll find a lot of activities related to the planets on this NASA website, including games, things to make, and animations to watch.

Ology
http://www.amnh.org/explore/ology/astronomy
This site sponsored by the American Museum of Natural History explores our place in space. Includes activities, games, and videos.

SpaceKids on Space.com
http://www.space.com/topics/spacekids-space-news-archive
This astronomy website for kids covers the solar system and beyond.

Answers

Puzzles
from pages 28 and 29

Close-up!
1. Jupiter's red spot
2. Saturn's rings
3. Sun's solar flare

Word jumble!
1. solar system
2. crater
3. moon
4. rings
5. lightning
6. astronaut

Match up!
1. a   2. d   3. e
4. f   5. b   6. c

True or false
from page 30

1. false
2. true
3. false
4. false
5. true

Index